Marino

by **Mark Stewart**

ACKNOWLEDGMENTS

The editors wish to thank Dan Marino for his cooperation in preparing this book. Thanks also to Integrated Sports International for their assistance.

PHOTO CREDITS

All photos courtesy AP/Wide World Photos, Inc. except the following:

Rich Kane/Sports Chrome – Cover, 6
Rob Tringali, Jr./Sports Chrome – 26, 27, 33, 46 top left, 47
Mark Stewart – 48

STAFF

Project Coordinator: John Sammis, Cronopio Publishing
Series Design Concept: The Sloan Group
Design and Electronic Page Makeup: Jaffe Enterprises, and
        Digital Communications Services, Inc.

LIBRARY OF CONGRESS CATALOGING-IN-PUBLICATION DATA

Stewart, Mark.
Dan Marino; A Grolier All-Pro Biography/ by Mark Stewart
        p. cm. – (Grolier all-pro biographies)
    Includes index.
    Summary: A brief biography of the well-known quarterback for the Miami Dolphins.
    ISBN 0-516-20167-0 (lib bdg.) 0-516-26030-8 (pbk.)
    1. Marino, Dan, 1961-   –Juvenile literature. 2. Football players–United States–
Biography–Juvenile literature. 3. Miami Dolphins (Football team)–Juvenile literature.
[1. Marino, Dan, 1961-   . 2. Football players.]
I. Title. II. Series.
GV939.M29S84 1996
796.332'092–dc20
    (B)
                                                                                    96-16096
                                                                                    CIP
                                                                                    AC

Grolier ALL-PRO Biographies™

Dan

Marino

by
Mark Stewart

CHILDREN'S PRESS®
A Division of Grolier Publishing
New York • London • Hong Kong • Sydney
Danbury, Connecticut

Contents

Who Am I? **6**

Growing Up. **8**

College Years. **14**

The Story Continues. **18**

Timeline **24**

Game Action! **26**

Dealing With It **30**

How Does He Do It? **32**

Family Matters **34**

Say What? **36**

Career Highlights **38**

Reaching Out **42**

Numbers **44**

What If **45**

Glossary **46**

Index **48**

Who

Am I?

When I was a kid, I knew I wanted to be a professional athlete. And for a long time, all I did was play sports. I didn't realize that doing well in school was part of the big picture. Luckily, I saw the light before it was too late. My name is Dan Marino, and this is my story . . . "

Growing Up

As far back as anyone can remember, Dan Marino always had a good arm. Growing up in the city of Pittsburgh, Pennsylvania, Dan always seemed to be throwing something. In the summer, it was a baseball; in the fall, it was a football; and in the winter, Dan was the winner of every neighborhood snowball fight. He would walk down the street, pick a target, and then launch a perfect spiral. He remembers, "I would take my football and start hitting things with passes—telephone poles, stop signs—even buses!" By the time he got to compete in his first tackle football game, everyone knew which position he would play—quarterback. And from that day forward, he has never played any other position.

What made Dan different from other good young athletes was that he sensed it takes more than natural ability to become a big-time quarterback. This is why he practiced all the time and worked to improve his skills.

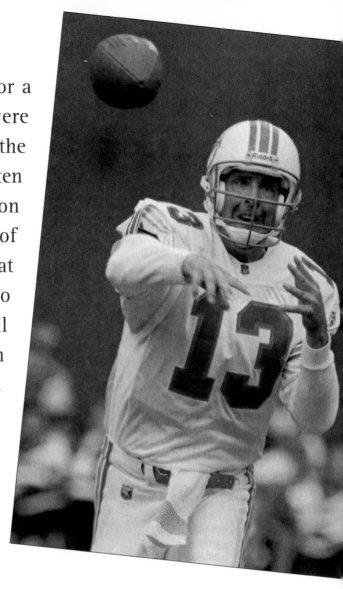

Dan Marino always had a great arm.

Dan's father drove a truck for a living. His deliveries were scheduled for very early in the morning, which meant that he often could return home in the afternoon to practice with Dan in front of their small, brick house or down at the local playground. He also taught Dan how to kick well enough to win the Pittsburgh Punt, Pass, and Kick contest. Dan's father also coached Dan's youth baseball and football teams. It was fun being the coach's son, although Dan's father made sure to treat him the same as the other boys. Sometimes, Dan actually got treated worse. For instance, when the kids selected jersey numbers, Dan's father told him that he would have to take any number that was left after his teammates had chosen. That number was "unlucky" 13—the lucky number Dan has worn ever since!

Terry Bradshaw, quarterback for the Pittsburgh Steelers, was Dan's childhood hero.

For a young boy who was crazy about sports, Pittsburgh was a wonderful place to grow up. The Steelers were building an NFL dynasty with their "Steel Curtain" defense and young quarterback Terry Bradshaw, who became Dan's hero. The Pirates were nearly as good, with superstars Roberto Clemente and Willie Stargell leading the team to the World Series in 1971. What Dan loved most was that you could see these players in the stores, in the supermarkets, and on the streets—they were not "gods," but real people. In fact, Stargell lived next door to Dan's grandmother, and Dan played some mean games of whiffle ball with the future Hall of Famer over the years.

Dan knew he wanted to be a famous athlete when he grew up. But at first he did not understand that, to achieve this goal, working hard in the classroom would be just as important as working hard on the field. Dan loved sports so much that he often forgot to do his homework. And although he could read as well as the other children in his class, he did not enjoy it.

Dan admits, "When I was young, all I wanted to do was be in the street playing ball all the time. I really didn't concentrate as much as I should have on my academics. My mother and father taught me that if I ever wanted to accomplish my dream of being a pro athlete, I had to do well in school. When I realized this, I did a lot better. And once I committed myself to learning and studying, I began to like reading, whether it was a school book or the sports section of the *Pittsburgh Gazette*, which is the newspaper my dad delivered. If you are having trouble reading, all I can say is work hard to improve and don't be afraid to ask for help. You must be able to read well just in order to get through life."

By the time Dan enrolled at Central Catholic High School, he had developed good study habits, especially when it came to taking notes in class. If the teacher said something important or wrote something on the blackboard, Dan was sure to jot it down. That way,

Pittsburgh Pirates captain Willie Stargell lived next door to Dan's grandmother.

he would be able to study for tests. This discipline also came in handy in football. Dan would take notes and write down his questions and ideas during the week, then study them before a game. He saw each game as a test, and he wanted to get the highest score possible.

Dan quickly became the star player of the football team, and he developed a reputation as an emotional leader. He would sometimes yell at his teammates if he felt they were not giving their best effort. They did not mind because Dan was even harder on himself. Dan was also an excellent baseball player. He pitched and played shortstop for Central, and he was the team's best hitter. He was so good at sports, in fact, that he was named the best high-school athlete in the state after his junior year.

When Dan started his senior year, he was considered by many to be the best young quarterback in the country. Dozens of college recruiters were knocking on his door. But Dan had his sights set on a school that was so close he could practically hit its campus with a long pass: the University of Pittsburgh. "There was no question where I wanted to go," he says. "I was just lucky that Pitt wanted me. There aren't many kids who can play major college football in front of their family and friends every week. I was very lucky."

Although Dan could have played for any college in the country, he chose Pittsburgh.

College

Dan Marino may have felt lucky to be attending a school where he could perform in front of his family and friends, but some critics were predicting that the combined pressure of playing close to home and quarterbacking a college team would get to him. Dan proved his doubters wrong by winning the starter's job after a few games and then handling it with maturity. As a freshman, Dan guided the Pittsburgh Panthers to a marvelous 10–1 season, and then edged the University of Arizona 16–10 in the Fiesta Bowl. When the final rankings were released, the University of Pittsburgh was among the top 10 teams in the nation.

Freshman Dan (right) and tight end Benjie Pryor get ready for the Fiesta Bowl.

Years

In his sophomore year, Dan led Pittsburgh to a 10–1 record.

In Dan's sophomore year, a serious knee injury threatened to end his season. But after just three games he limped back into the lineup and led Pitt to another 10–1 record. After winning the Gator Bowl, Pitt finished second in the national rankings.

In spite of his bad knee, Dan worked to achieve mental and physical skills that are rare in a college quarterback. Before taking the snap, he could glance at a defense and instantly recognize what the other team was about to do. Even more impressive was that Dan could react to what he saw and bark out a brand new play right at the line of scrimmage—something that many pro quarterbacks never learn to do.

Great things were predicted for Dan as his junior year began, but no one could have foreseen the kind of season he would have. He threw for 2,615 yards and 34 touchdowns to lead Pittsburgh to its third straight 10–1 season. In the Sugar Bowl, Dan engineered a dramatic, come-from-behind win over Georgia. His 33-yard touchdown strike to tight end John Brown with less than a minute left was his 26th completion in just 41 attempts that day, and it earned Dan the game's MVP award. Again, the Panthers finished as the second-ranked team in the country. Thanks to his wonderful season, Dan was named to several All-America squads.

Dan diagrams the play that helped him set a school record for passing in his junior year.

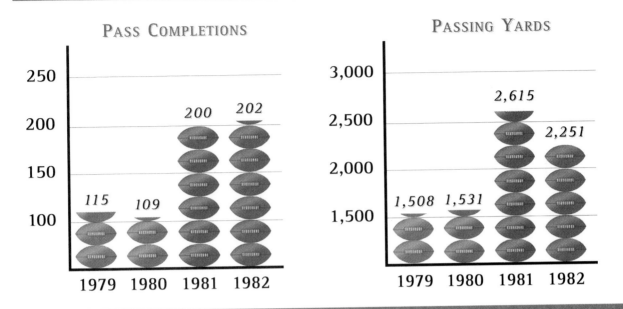

PASS COMPLETIONS

250

200 — 202

150

115 — 109

100

1979 1980 1981 1982

PASSING YARDS

3,000

2,615

2,500 — 2,251

2,000

1,508 1,531

1,500

1979 1980 1981 1982

Dan's final year at the University of Pittsburgh was somewhat disappointing. The team slipped to 9–2, and played poorly in a 7–3 Cotton Bowl loss. Dan's stats were excellent, but not as good as the year before. On the bright side, he had completed the requirements for his degree in communications, and did well enough in class to be nominated as an Academic All-American.

As pro scouts tried to analyze Dan's senior season, they asked some troubling questions. Had Dan's football career already peaked? Was his junior season a fluke? Was his knee completely healed? That would be left for the NFL to decide. In a draft packed with promising college quarterbacks, Dan no longer looked like the best of the bunch.

The Story

On the day of the 1983 NFL draft, Dan Marino watched as teams called the name of one quarterback after another. He was shocked that his name was not among the first few. The Miami Dolphins were equally shocked. Miami had the next-to-last pick in the first round. When their turn came, they chose Dan. Miami coach Don Shula knew he had picked

The Los Angeles Express chose Dan with the first pick in the United States Football League draft, but he chose to play for Miami in the NFL.

Continues

someone special. When the young quarterback first met the famous coach, Marino told Shula, "All I want is to be the best quarterback in the NFL. And I'll do whatever you want me to do to be that."

The first thing Coach Shula wanted Dan to do was to be patient. The Dolphins already had a talented young quarterback named David Woodley. He had led the team to the Super Bowl a season earlier. Dan would have to wait, watch, and learn so he would be ready to play when the time came. It might mean a season on the bench, Shula told him, or it could be even longer.

As it turned out, Dan spent less than a month watching from the sidelines. In two of the team's first four 1983 contests, he came in and guided the Dolphins to quick scores after Woodley had failed to move the ball. Prior to the season's sixth game, Shula decided that Dan's strong arm and quick release made up for his inexperience, and he was named the starter. Suddenly, the Dolphin offense caught fire. After putting five touchdowns on the board in a loss to the Buffalo Bills, Dan went on to win 9 of the final 10 games! Though just a rookie, he finished the year as the top-rated passer in the American Football Conference (AFC), and guided the Dolphins to the

Dan escapes the San Francisco 49er rush during the 1985 Super Bowl.

second-best record in all of football. NFL fans did not realize it, but they had just seen an early glimpse of a football legend.

Dan started to set new standards for quarterbacks in just his second year in the league. In 1984, he not only led the NFL in passes completed, passing yards, and touchdowns, he broke the old records in each category! Hooking up with receivers Mark Clayton and Mark Duper, Dan proved unstoppable all season long. He led the Dolphins to victory in their first 11 games, then won three out of the next five to tie the team record of 14 victories. In the playoffs, Dan scorched the Seattle Seahawks 31–10, then overwhelmed the Pittsburgh Steelers 45–28 to win the AFC championship. In his first full season as a starting quarterback, Dan had made it to the Super Bowl. Against the San Francisco 49ers, Dan was magnificent in the early going, but several bad plays by the punting unit robbed the Dolphins of their momentum. Down 38–16 and

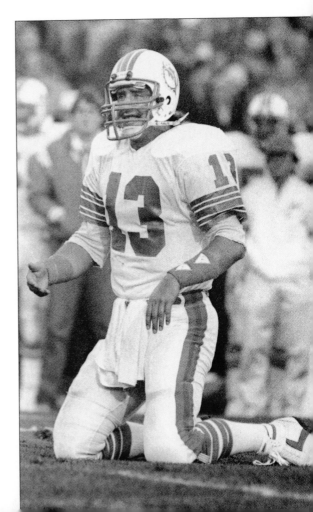

Dan kneels in anguish as his Dolphins fall apart in Super Bowl XIX.

forced to pass on nearly every play, Dan was unable to rally Miami to victory. Dan was heartbroken about the loss, but he figured that he would have a few more chances to win a Super Bowl during his career.

Those chances never came. Although Dan went on to break almost every single-season and career passing mark in NFL history, the Dolphins never again made it to the big game. "When you go to the Super Bowl at age 23, you don't realize how tough it is to get there," he says. "Now I know."

Other than not winning a Super Bowl, Dan has had a fabulous career. Most experts consider him to be the best passer of all time, and many of his records may stand forever. In a 1995 game against the New England Patriots, Dan connected with receiver Irving Fryar on a nine-yard completion to break the NFL career record for passing yards. He had already shattered the record for completions five weeks earlier, and by season's end he would set new standards for career attempts and touchdown passes. Now, every time Dan licks his fingers, takes the snap from center, and drops back to pass, he is rewriting the record books.

Dan acknowledges the fans after breaking the all-time NFL record for passing yards.

Timeline

1979: Enrolls at University of Pittsburgh

1983: Joins NFL Miami Dolphins

1981: Leads Pitt to number-two national ranking for second straight year

24

1995: Breaks four all-time NFL passing records

1984: Leads Dolphins to 14–2 record and appearance in the Super Bowl

1986: Completes career-high 378 passes

Game

Dan's 343 yards against the Atlanta Falcons in a 1995 game enabled him to break the all-time record for career 300-yard passing games.

Losing the Super Bowl in his second pro season still sticks with Dan as a major disappointment. "I don't want to walk away from the game without winning a Super Bowl . . . the records and awards are nice, but being there at the end is really what it's all about."

Action!

Dan has thrown a touchdown in each of his 12 post-season appearances. His record-setting streak is still active going into 1996.

Dan has topped 20 touchdowns a record 12 times in his career. The next-best mark is 8, by Hall of Famer Johnny Unitas. Dan says, "There is no substitute for throwing the ball well—it is the most important skill you can have at my position."

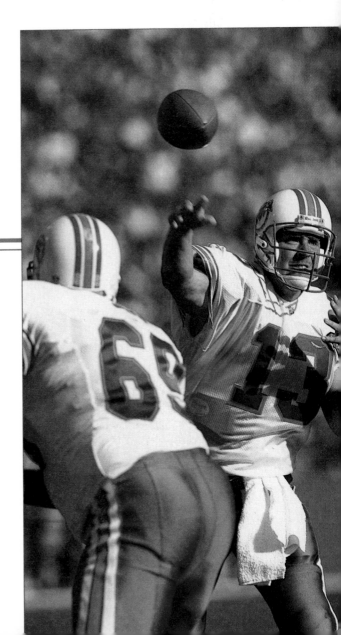

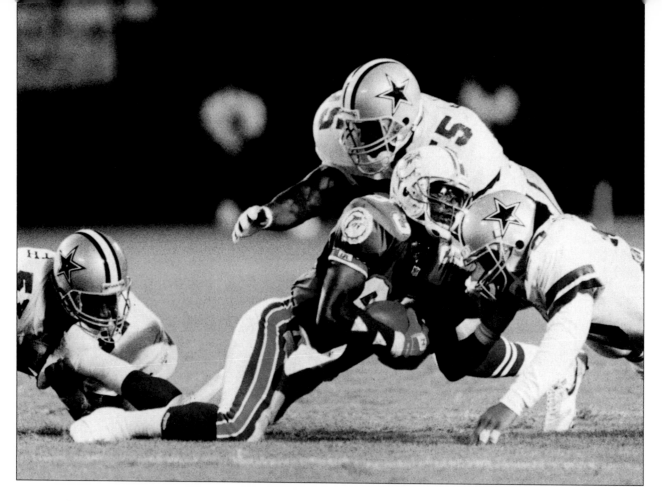

Dan's favorite receiver was Mark Clayton (with ball). They connected for 79 touchdowns.

Dan thinks people don't give him enough credit for being fast on his feet. "I'm quick enough in the pocket to make people miss, and give me a little more time to throw."

Dan started more games for coach Don Shula than any other quarterback, including Hall of Famers Bob Griese and Johnny Unitas. "I am most proud of the fact that I have been consistently played at a high level from year to year."

Dan and coach Don Shula discuss strategy.

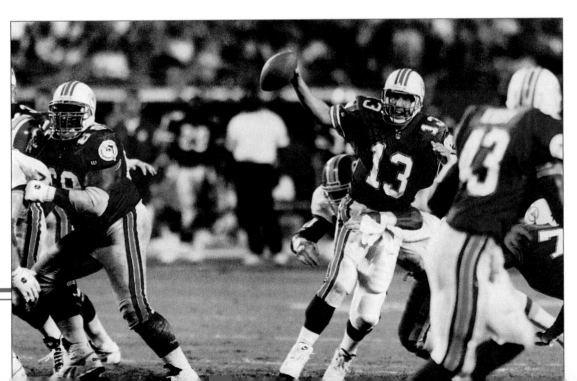

Dealing

October 10, 1993, was a dark day for the Miami Dolphins. After playing 145 consecutive games, Dan Marino was lying on the turf at Joe Robbie Stadium with a torn Achilles tendon. It was a season-ending injury suffered on a day when the offense had really come together for the first time that season. In Dan's absence, back-up quarterback Scott Mitchell played well, causing some to wonder whether Dan was worth

Dan is examined by the team trainer after his 1993 Achilles tendon injury.

With It

keeping in 1994—even if he managed to make a full recovery!

"It was not an easy situation to deal with. First of all, I never thought I would get hurt. Playing for so many years without any major problems, you have a false sense of security. So I decided that the best way to respond was by focusing on my rehab and on making a complete comeback. I knew if I could do that, everything else would take care of itself. With hard work and dedication, I was back practicing in about five months. And when the 1994 season started, I was back at quarterback for the Dolphins."

Dan tests his repaired tendon during training camp before the 1994 season.

How Does

Dan Marino has as much natural ability as any passer who has ever played football. But what has made him great is that he has a tremendous awareness of the playing field and the game situation. This skill enables him to act immediately when he spots an opportunity, even if it is there for a split second. In the final moments of a 1994 game against the New York Jets, everyone assumed that Dan was going to spike the ball to stop the clock. But when he saw New York's defenders relax, he took the snap and—before anyone realized what he was doing—whipped a 14-yard touchdown pass to a wide-open Mark Ingram to win the game!

"I know I have been blessed with a great talent, so the challenge for me is to find new ways to make it work for the team. In this game, it's not always enough to keep your body in shape . . . you also have to exercise your mind."

Dan spots a weakness in the Jets' defense and calls an audible.

He Do It?

Family

Matters

Dan and Claire Marino have four children, Daniel III, Michael, Joseph, and Alexandra. Dan has made a lot of friends in football, but he still considers his father to be his best buddy.

"You know, it's funny. I had a lot of friends growing up, but I ended up with my dad being my best friend. He helped me get through a lot of situations when I was younger, in sports and in life."

Dan's parents, Veronica and Dan Sr., hug in front of a wall where Dan's magazine covers are hung.

Say What?

Here's what football people are saying about Dan Marino:

"Everybody has tried everything they know to slow him down, but he's done things that nobody has ever done before."

—*Don Shula, former Dolphins coach*

"His spirals always found me in full stride."

—*Mark Duper, former teammate*

"Regardless of your defense, Dan will find a way to punch a hole in it."

—*Chuck Noll, former Pittsburgh Steelers coach*

"The only time I enjoy watching him is when he's sitting on the bench!"

—*Marv Levy, Buffalo Bills coach*

"Marino has a gun of an arm, but it's the mental aspect of his game that scares me."

—*Ron Meyer,*
  former Colts coach

"We constantly look for ways to stop Marino. We haven't found any yet."

—*Joe Walton,*
  former Jets coach

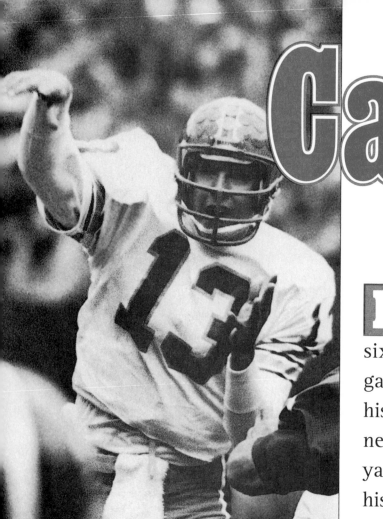

Career

Dan broke University of Pittsburgh records with six touchdown passes in a game, 37 in a season, and 79 in his career. He also established new marks with 2,876 passing yards in a season, and 8,416 for his four-year career.

Dan adds to his Pittsburgh passing records against Rutgers.

Dan has been selected to play in nine Pro Bowls.

Dan has won 122 games in his career—by far the most for a Dolphins quarterback.

Highlights

Dan holds his 1984 NFL Most Valuable Player trophy.

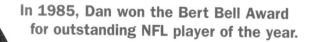

In 1985, Dan won the Bert Bell Award
for outstanding NFL player of the year.

In 1983, Dan was the NFL Rookie of the Year; in 1984, he won Player of the Year honors.

Dan passed for 40,000 career yards faster than any quarterback in history, taking just 153 games to reach that plateau.

Dan leads
the AFC in
the 1993
Pro Bowl.

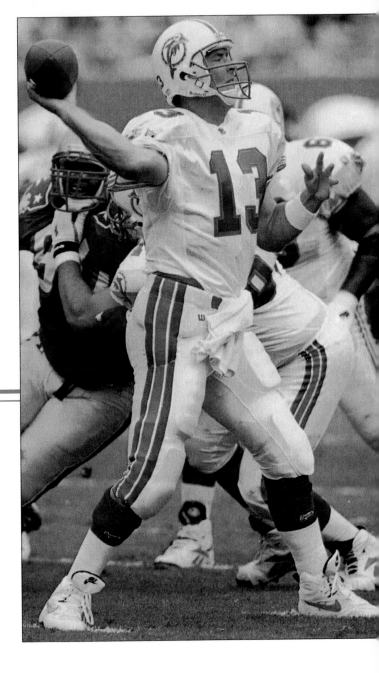

After the 1995 season, Dan had set NFL career passing records of 6,531 attempts, 3,913 completions, 48,441 yards, and 352 touchdown passes.

Dan throws the pass that breaks the record of 47,003 career passing yards held by Fran Tarkenton.

Dan has topped the NFL in pass completions five times. No quarterback has ever led the league more often.

Reaching

Dan Marino has been involved with charity work since the day he became a Miami Dolphin. Over the years, he has given his time, money, and advice to countless organizations. He even has his own foundation, which has raised more than $2 million for children's charities in south Florida.

There is one cause, however, that has become very close to his heart. A few years ago, doctors told Dan and Claire that their son, Michael, had a mild case of autism. Autism is a disorder that makes it hard for Michael to react and communicate the way other kids do. The Marinos found a great school for Michael, and have raised money for the school to make sure that Michael and his friends have everything they need.

"He's doing incredibly well and has a chance to go through school and be like a normal child."

Out

Dan and fellow NFL quarterback Jack Trudeau appear
at a benefit for the Tomorrow's Children Fund.

Numbers

Name: Daniel Constantine Marino Jr.

Born: September 15, 1961

Height: 6' 4"

Weight: 225 pounds

Uniform Number: 13

College: University
of Pittsburgh

Dan's string of 10 straight seasons with 20 or more touchdown passes is the longest in NFL history.

Year	Team	Games	Attempts	Completions	Yards	Pct.	TD Passes	QB Rating
1983	Miami Dolphins	11	296	173	2,210	58.4	20	96.0
1984	Miami Dolphins	16	564*	362*	5,084*	64.2	48*	108.9*
1985	Miami Dolphins	16	567	336*	4,137*	59.3	30*	84.1
1986	Miami Dolphins	16	623*	378*	4,746*	60.7	44*	92.5
1987	Miami Dolphins	12	444	263	3,245	59.2	26	89.2
1988	Miami Dolphins	16	606*	354*	4,434*	58.4	28	80.8
1989	Miami Dolphins	16	550	308	3,997	56.0	24	76.9
1990	Miami Dolphins	16	531	306	3,563	57.6	21	82.6
1991	Miami Dolphins	16	549	318	3,970	57.9	25	85.8
1992	Miami Dolphins	16	554*	330*	4,116*	59.6	24	85.1
1993	Miami Dolphins	5	150	91	1,218	60.7	8	95.9
1994	Miami Dolphins	16	615	385	4,453	62.6	30	89.2
1995	Miami Dolphins	14	482	309	3,668	64.1	24	90.8
Totals		186	6,531	3,913	48,441	59.9	352	88.4

* Led league

What If...

When I was in college, some people worried that my knee might not hold up to the punishment it would get in the NFL. Had they been right— had I been forced from the game—I believe I would have gone into broadcasting, or maybe even acting. At the University of Pittsburgh, I learned a lot about the business and received my degree in communications. I also learned that, whatever you do, the key to success is working hard and having fun while you're doing it."

Glossary

COMMUNICATIONS the study of how people relate to each other

CONSECUTIVE several events that follow one after another

ACADEMIC concerning education and learning

ACHILLES TENDON the strong tissues that join the muscles in the calf of the leg to the bone of the heel

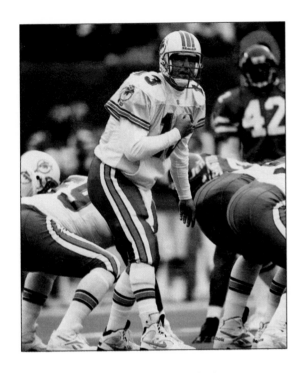

PLATEAU a level of high accomplishment

RECRUITER one who tries to get people to join their team or organization

"STEEL CURTAIN" nickname for the Pittsburgh Steelers' magnificent defense during the 1970s

DYNASTY a powerful team or group that maintains its position for a long time

FLUKE a one-time occurrence; an accident of good luck

LACKLUSTER without brilliance or vitality; dull

MOMENTUM strength or force gained by motion or through the development of events

Index

Atlanta Falcons, 26

Bradshaw, Terry, 10

Brown, John, 16

Buffalo Bills, 20, 37

Central Catholic High School, 11–12

Clayton, Mark, 21, 28

Clemente, Roberto, 10

Cotton Bowl, 17

Duper, Mark, 21, 36

Fiesta Bowl, 14

Fryar, Irving, 22

Gator Bowl, 15

Griese, Bob, 29

Ingram, Mark, 32

Joe Robbie Stadium, 30

Levy, Marv, 37

Marino, Dan
  and awards/honors, 16, 17, 38, 39, 40, 41
  childhood of, 8–13
  education of, 10–12, 17, 45
  family of, 9, 11, 35, 42
  and football records, 21, 22, 26, 27, 38, 40, 41
  uniform number of, 9

Meyer, Ron, 37

Miami Dolphins, 18–23, 30, 31, 36, 38, 42

Mitchell, Scott, 30

New England Patriots, 22

New York Jets, 32, 37

Noll, Chuck, 36

Pittsburgh Pirates, 10

Pittsburgh Gazette, 11

Pittsburgh, Pennsylvania, 8

Pittsburgh Steelers, 9, 10, 21, 36

Pryor, Benji, 14

Punt, Pass, and Kick, 9

San Francisco 49ers, 20, 21

Seattle Seahawks, 21

Shula, Don, 18–19, 20, 29, 36

Stargell, Willie, 10, 11

Sugar Bowl, 16

Super Bowl, 19, 21–22, 26

Tomorrow's Children Fund, 43

Trudeau, Jack, 43

Unitas, Johnny, 27, 29

University of Arizona, 14

University of Pittsburgh, 12, 14–17, 16, 38

Walton, Joe, 37

Woodley, David, 19, 20

World Series, 10

About The Author

Mark Stewart grew up in New York City in the 1960s and 1970s—when the Mets, Jets, and Knicks all had championship teams. As a child, Mark read everything about sports he could lay his hands on. Today, he is one of the busiest sportswriters around. Since 1990, he has written close to 500 sports stories for kids, including profiles on more than 200 athletes, past and present. A graduate of Duke University, Mark served as senior editor of *Racquet*, a national tennis magazine, and was managing editor of *Super News*, a sporting goods industry newspaper. He is the author of every Grolier All-Pro Biography.